KATHERINE SOPER

Katherine Soper wrote *The Small Hours* for National Theatre
Connections 2019. Her other work includes *Loose Lips* (Big
House) and *Wish List* (Royal Exchange/Royal Court), for which
she won the 2015 Bruntwood Prize for Playwriting, the 2017
Stage Debut Award for Best Writer, and was shortlisted for the
Evening Standard Most Promising Playwright Award.

Katherine Soper

THE SMALL HOURS

NICK HERN BOOKS

London

www.nickhernbooks.co.uk

A Nick Hern Book

The Small Hours first published in Great Britain in 2020 as a paperback original by Nick Hern Books Limited, The Glasshouse, 49a Goldhawk Road, London W12 8QP

The Small Hours copyright © 2020 Katherine Soper

Katherine Soper has asserted her right to be identified as the author of this work

Cover image: © Shutterstock.com/UNIKYLUCKK

Designed and typeset by Nick Hern Books, London
Printed in Great Britain by Mimeo Ltd, Huntingdon, Cambridgeshire PE29 6XX

ISBN 978 1 84842 896 6

A CIP catalogue record for this book is available from the British Library

The drink you spilt all over me
Lover's Spit left on repeat
My mom and dad let me stay home
It drives you crazy getting old

This dream isn't feeling sweet
We're reeling through the midnight streets
And I've never felt more alone
It feels so scary getting old

Lorde, 2013, aged sixteen

I know this much: that there is objective time, but
also subjective time, the time you wear on the
inside of your wrist, next to where the pulse lies.

Julian Barnes, 2011, aged sixty-five

The Small Hours was commissioned as part of the 2019
National Theatre Connections Festival and premiered by youth
theatres across the UK, including a performance at the National
Theatre in June 2019.

Each year the National Theatre asks ten writers to create new
plays to be performed by young theatre companies all over the
country. From Scotland to Cornwall and Northern Ireland to
Norfolk, Connections celebrates great new writing for the stage –
and the energy, commitment and talent of young theatremakers.

www.nationaltheatre.org.uk/connections

Note on Play

The first four scenes are set on the Friday night (or, technically, Saturday morning) of May half-term.

The final scene is everything after that.

A line across the page in the final scene indicates a new 'unit'. Even though it's all one scene, these units are like miniature scenes within it.

When there is a dash instead of a character's name, this indicates somebody speaking who isn't one of the eight named characters. It's mostly up to you who that is, though if you choose to have actors playing multiple roles, it should be clear that the dash speaker isn't one of the original eight characters.

I've kept the locations vague – an island, a city, the suburbs, the sticks – in the hope that you can pin them down in locations that work well for you.

Even where a character's gender is specified, I originally wrote all these characters gender-blind, with the intention and hope that they could be performed in any combination. Any dialogue that seems to nail down a gender for a character can easily be cut or adapted as you see fit.

K.S.

Characters

EPI
PEEBS
JAZZ
RED
JAFFA
KEESH
VJ
WOLFIE

Before the first scene

If you want, it could be nice to have all the characters onstage together, so we have some idea of who we're going to meet over the course of the play – some idea of the night that's going to unfold. Otherwise…

1 a.m.

An island

A music-practice room in a school. EPI*'s in their dressing gown – it's probably pretty old and tatty – and they have an instrument of some sort. In my mind it's a cello but pretty much any instrument would work – they don't necessarily have to be good at it.*

EPI *prepares to play – adjusting his music stand, posture, tuning, etc – and then starts to play a tune. Once he goes wrong a few times and can't fix it, he gives up and start playing random notes.*

PEEBS *enters, boots caked in mud, carrying a holdall. He lingers by the door silently for a bit, listening, out of* EPI*'s sight.*

PEEBS. Nah that's *definitely* not right.

EPI Hey. Hi.

Sorry were you –

He notices PEEBS*' clothes.*

– you weren't asleep.

PEEBS. It's early.

EPI *wavers for a moment between whether he should keep playing or say something else.*

You play that like every weekend, I can hear you from my room.

EPI. Well. Yeah. I have to practise sometime.

Beat.

Er. Where's your room?

PEEBS. ...Ketterley.

EPI. Oh. Obviously. Yeah.

PEEBS. So on weekends I'm hearing you play – I don't know, whatever that was – and in the week I've got Skinny up there listening to hardcore trance while he revises.

EPI. ...I can shut the window if you want.

PEEBS. It's fine, it's better than the trance. Not that I've got anything against that stuff, just, you know. I wouldn't choose to revise to it.

Pause.

PEEBS *takes off his boots and starts hitting the sides on the floor, or any other available surface, to get the mud off.*

EPI *tries to do some quiet tuning of his instrument, but the noise of* PEEBS' *boots is a bit too distracting.*

What time have you got?

EPI. Huh?

PEEBS. Time.

EPI. Um. One.

PEEBS *makes a kind of 'hmm' sound.*

What?

PEEBS. No, I've got the same.

Pause.

PEEBS *starts bashing his boots again*.

I swear it feels like it's morning already.

EPI. Yeah?

PEEBS. Doesn't it feel like it should be later to you?

EPI. Maybe. I dunno.

Peebs, did you… like, need something?

PEEBS (*indicating his boot*). D'you mind me doing this?

EPI. I mean. Not like this is my bedroom.

PEEBS. I'll try and do it in the bin.

Pause as he finds the bin and starts scraping the dried mud in there instead.

I'm having an operation on Monday.

EPI. …okay.

PEEBS. And so I was meant to be going to Ash's for the weekend so I get in, like, two days of actual half-term cos I'm gonna have to stay in bed for the rest of it.

Beat.

EPI. Right.

PEEBS. But Ash runs off really quickly after Chemistry and I'm like, what the hell you're meant to be taking me back to yours – so I end up walking around on the pitch for like *hours* I swear, holding my phone like this to get signal so I can call him – and when I get through he's like, *'Hi, how are you'*, like a total freak – and he's already on the ferry – and for ages he actually pretends he's forgotten I was even meant to be staying.

Turns out his mum's banned anyone from coming over. Wanna know why?

EPI. Why?

PEEBS. House isn't clean.

Beat.

EPI. Really?

PEEBS. Yep.

EPI....but you wouldn't care / about

PEEBS. Oh. I know. I know. But.

PEEBS *shrugs.*

EPI. That's wank.

PEEBS. Why do parents care about stuff like that? Like even if it was dirty enough for me to notice, which I bet it's not, like, she should see my room – who does she think I'm even gonna tell?!

EPI. Your mum.

PEEBS. What, all the way over in Texas? Good luck.

PEEBS *lies down on the floor in irritation, before popping back up and pulling a jumper out of his holdall. He puts it on and lies back down.*

So, yeah, I'm actually just stuck here now.

And I saw Mr Marcello in the corridor like three times and every single time he's like, '*Ohhh here you are again*', and it's like. Get away from me.

EPI. Oh. Yeah. This is why I hide out here.

PEEBS. I can't believe he lives here out of choice. It's just weird.

Beat.

EPI. Y'know, no one here even told me there was gonna be another person staying when you went full-time.

PEEBS. I'd say I'm shocked but that's like the least shocking thing I've ever heard.

EPI. I kinda got – used to it being just me.

PEEBS. I'm never gonna be used to this. Everywhere's so quiet it's creepy, I tried to eat in the hall once and just wanted to throw something.

Sorry if you wanted the company.

EPI. I don't eat there either.

PEEBS. Oh.

EPI. I don't like, sit there all pathetic on my own in the hall, why would I do that?

PEEBS. Okay, okay.

EPI. Like you do know why I'm called Epi, right?

PEEBS (*as if he's only just thought about it for the first time*)....no.

EPI. Cos back in Year 3 I was the only one in school with an EpiPen.

PEEBS *laughs for a second, before saying:*

PEEBS. I forgot you've been here that long! No wonder you bloody live here, mate.

EPI. Uh –

EPI *decides not to take the bait there, and carries on.*

Yeah, so they did like a whole long thing in assembly about all the things I'm allergic to and what to do if I went into anaphylactic shock.

So I don't eat in the hall even in the week. Way too many nut particles.

PEEBS. Is it just nuts?

EPI. And like, everything else pretty much. Fish and milk and eggs. And bee stings.

PEEBS. *Milk?*

EPI. ...a bit, yeah.

PEEBS. Have you ever eaten any of it by accident? And like your face swelled up or something??

EPI. Uh, once. In the infant school. That's why they did the whole assembly thing.

PEEBS. What was it like?

EPI. I mean. Like, horrible, I never want it to happen again, but it was kinda exciting. I had a bunk bed at hospital.

It'll be fine, y'know.

PEEBS. What?

EPI. Your operation.

PEEBS. You don't even know what I'm getting done. And plus you hear all that stuff about people who the anaesthetic doesn't totally take for them and they can feel everything but they can't move or speak or let the doctors know or anything.

Beat. EPI *doesn't quite know what to say to that.*

It's a cyst I'm getting removed.

EPI. Oh. Right. Jesus.

PEEBS. Sounds so dramatic, it's meant to be really safe.

EPI. Okay.

PEEBS. But like I said, everyone says that.

Beat.

I had a dream that it like, burst. My cyst. And I got a magnifying glass or something and looked inside and I could see all my flesh in layers and all this pus bubbling inside it like a volcano or something. And it had teeth.

EPI. Teeth?

PEEBS. Yeah, like, all these little baby teeth around the edges?

EPI. That's gross.

PEEBS. Yeah, I know.

EPI. What is a cyst anyway? Is it pus inside?

PEEBS. I dunno, I think it's some kind of liquid. The doctor kept calling it a *sac* when he talked about it and that just really grossed me out so I think that's why I had the dream.

EPI. Y'know my dad had about five different operations last year. And he was actually pretty okay. Apparently they're, nurses are like trained to be really good before operations, especially if you tell them you're worried.

Beat.

PEEBS. Okay.

EPI. Dunno if that's helpful.

PEEBS. I'm not actually worried.

EPI. You kinda sounded like you were.

PEEBS. I'm not. Just I can't believe I'm basically not gonna get a half-term now.

EPI. Maybe everyone will come and visit you.

PEEBS. Would you come back here, of your own free will, once you got to the mainland for a week?

EPI. ...maybe not.

PEEBS. Yeah.

Pause.

EPI. What's Texas like?

PEEBS. Hot. I can't really go out much there cos I burn really easily even with suncream.

I went to NASA last time though, that was cool.

EPI. You can drive when you're sixteen over there.

PEEBS. Yeah.

EPI. Do you reckon if one of us got a car when we turn
seventeen they'd let us keep it here? And like… go places?

PEEBS. Where would you go though? The stone circles?
Yaaaay. Not like I've seen those five million times already.

Beat.

Not sure what else to do, EPI *distracts himself with his
instrument. He plays the song he was playing at the start of
the scene – times it on his phone – and it only lasts about
twenty seconds, if that. He looks at the timer, dispirited.*

EPI. I don't think I'm ever gonna finish this.

PEEBS. What?

EPI. Composition unit. Like I thought I might get it done
tonight cos I couldn't get to sleep, but. Three minutes is
actually ages. Like if you actually time it, it's so long.

PEEBS. Yeah. So what're you gonna do?

EPI. I should probably just take some Sominex and try and get
to sleep.

*He starts to put his instrument away. Once he's finished and
is about to leave:*

Nice talking to you, Peebs.

Beat.

PEEBS. Yeah. Yeah.

…might actually go for a smoke, thinking about it.

PEEBS *starts pulling his boots on again.*

They come out into the open air.

PEEBS *starts to fish a cigarette out of a crumpled pack
somewhere in his pocket.*

Hang on, you're not allergic to smoke, are you?

EPI….no.

PEEBS. Okay, just checking before you start like, foaming at the mouth or whatever.

EPI. I don't have rabies.

PEEBS (*laughing*). Oh yeah! Yeah, I'm thinking of rabies.

Comfortable pause.

Where do your parents live again?

EPI. Er. China.

PEEBS. Wow.

EPI. Yeah.

PEEBS. ...do you wish you'd moved there too?

EPI. Um. Kinda just think he should have stayed here in the first place.

PEEBS. Yeah. Same.

Beat.

If I had kids, I would never do that to them. Ever. Just fuck off and like...

PEEBS *breaks off, surprised by himself. He's said all this with such force that both of them are a bit taken aback.*

So PEEBS *checks his phone, holding it out to try and find signal.*

You probably wanna sleep.

EPI. I mean. Yeah, but.

If I don't sleep through tomorrow I might as well, I dunno – go down to the sea. Not that there's anything interesting out there but. Could try and flag down a ferry.

PEEBS. Tomorrow?

EPI. Yeah.

PEEBS. ...All right. Let's do that.

EPI. Okay.

PEEBS. My door's the one right by the fire escape. Just bang really loudly if I don't hear.

EPI. Okay. Yeah. I'll do that.

EPI *leaves*.

PEEBS *tries again with the lighter – no dice. He sighs a bit, and plonks himself down. He might feel his cyst, wherever it is… he checks his phone… nothing doing there either.*

Time passes slowly.

2 a.m.

A city

RED *and* JAZZ *are walking together, eating chips*.

RED. You know who's banging now?

JAZZ. Who?

RED. Col and Hannah.

JAZZ. NO. Are you shitting me? Oh my god.

   …I shared a *sofa* with them!

RED. What, at his house?

JAZZ. Yeah!

RED. Covered in jizz now.

JAZZ. NO. Oh my god. How did – this doesn't compute, this makes literally no sense to me.

RED. Yeah, but they don't know I know, they think it's some big secret, so – shh.

JAZZ. Ugh. Sorry, I need to go and delete this whole conversation from my brain or I'm gonna have horrible disturbing dreams later.

RED. You're so welcome.

Beat.

JAZZ. This is me.

RED. This is – oh okay. I didn't know we were –

Wait, is your dad in?

JAZZ. No, he's – on a date, I think.

RED. Oh. Right. Can I see your digs?

JAZZ. Sure. Yeah.

JAZZ *lets* RED *into her bedroom.*

RED. You got your own private loo?!

JAZZ. Yeah.

RED. That's mad.

JAZZ. Why?

RED. You don't even have to have, like, morning strategy now.

JAZZ. Ohhh. Yeah, forgot about that.

RED. Give us a look then.

RED *checks out* JAZZ*'s en suite.*

How's Papa Bear?

JAZZ. Yeah, he's all right.

RED. Do you think he'd mind if I called him Papa Bear?

JAZZ. He'd probably think it was weird that you decided to start now.

RED *laughs.*

RED. Yeah.

On a date, eh?

Must be having a good night.

JAZZ *shrugs*.

Pause.

Where has he taken her? Pryzm?

JAZZ. I don't like, *ask* him what he's doing.

RED. I bet you if we go down there now – it's still open, we'll find them like, plastered on the ground next to one of the ambulances.

JAZZ *doesn't find this as funny as* RED *expects her to*.

Beat as RED *tries to think of something else to talk about*.

You know the last time we saw each other was that time in Subway.

JAZZ. – oh yeah!

RED. Six months ago.

JAZZ. Was it actually six months?

RED. Yeah. It was November.

JAZZ. Wow.

RED. I feel, like, completely different now.

JAZZ.Your hair is different.

RED. Yeah. Shouldn't even be called Red any more.

Y'know, Mum says that if you and Milla still want her to cut your hair you can just pop round and she'll do it.

JAZZ. Would that – ?

RED. Free, obviously.

I dunno, I think she'd like to see you.

Pause. RED *picks up a medal that's carefully nestled somewhere in* JAZZ's *room.*

This is fun, when'd you win this?

JAZZ. Last term.

RED *puts it on.*

RED. Does it suit me?

JAZZ. Um –

RED. I'm kidding.

Takes it off, gives it back.

Still running then.

JAZZ. Yeah. Yeah. Mostly long distance now.

RED. That's good.

JAZZ. I'm going to this sports camp thing for it.

RED. Really? In summer?

JAZZ. Yeah.

RED. Okay.

JAZZ. The people who run it came to the, um, the event I won, and they asked if I wanted to come.

RED. Oh, right.

Well done!

JAZZ. Thanks.

RED. What do you do at camps like that? Just… train really hard all day?

JAZZ. I guess so, that's what they're for.

RED. What do you do when it rains?

JAZZ. Same thing.

RED. Can I come?

Beat.

JAZZ....

RED. You don't want me to. That's fine.

JAZZ. No, like...

Why d'you say stuff like that?

RED. I dunno.

JAZZ. You do, you always get this weird look. Like you know you're taking the piss.

RED. I think I just – really enjoy being all – you know how you sometimes get this vision of something you *could* do or say? And it's really rude or inappropriate?

JAZZ....yeah...

RED. I just do it. I can't help it. Like what's-her-face, Tanya from year below was walking down the corridor this week balancing loads of things on her and I just had this vision of like – batting the stuff out of her hands. So I just did it. And she was really pissed off about it, like, obviously, and on one hand I felt really bad cos it was such a dick move but then I also kinda couldn't stop laughing cos somehow I also found it really funny.

RED *might even laugh in the telling.*

JAZZ. And what happened?

RED. Nothing. Got put on report again.

JAZZ. Oh. Right.

RED. What?

JAZZ. Nothing. Just thought you were getting better is all.

RED. Oh my god, Jazz. You literally sound like my teacher right now.

JAZZ. All right, all right.

RED. Why do you think I wanna hear comments like that? From you?

JAZZ. Red –

RED. No –

JAZZ. C'mere –

RED. Oh my god – no – like – don't bloody *hug me* now –

JAZZ. You wanna wear my medal? Will that help?

RED. Don't be stupid, I don't actually want it.

JAZZ. Go on.

RED. No. Fuck off.

JAZZ. Hey.

RED. No, just seriously do not touch me right now when I asked you not to touch me, okay?

JAZZ. ...you're a real dick you know that?

RED. Fucking –

JAZZ. I'd forgotten what a dick you are / but you really are.

RED. You literally have no idea what you're talking about, you're not even around any more so don't go fucking telling me *I'm* a dick all right – I am having to literally stop myself from laying into you right now so don't / *push* me –

JAZZ (*hands up*). Okay! Okay okay!

Pause.

RED. Oh my *days*.

I should probably go cos I still feel like I'm gonna punch something or – I'm just kinda – (*Does some sort of gesture to mean 'freaking out'.*) right now.

JAZZ. Maybe you need to – breathe – Like really deep and slow – / like

RED. *I know how to breathe!!*

> JAZZ *demonstrates*. RED *manages to join in*.
>
> *Pause*.

> If you weren't family I would actually have hit you.

JAZZ. Yeah well I'd probably have hit you back, wouldn't I?

RED. You'd have tried.

> All that running and I swear you've not got any muscles.
>
> *Pause*.
>
> Jazz, I'm just telling you in advance I reckon I might need to vom in your nice toilet later.

JAZZ. Oh. Was it the ke/bab?

RED. Dunno. Don't matter.

JAZZ. D'you want some water?

> RED *shakes her head*.
>
> *Pause*.

RED. Milla's not here.

JAZZ. Yeah, she's proper cabin crew now. So she's always in Dubai or asleep.

RED. Cool. She's doing what she wanted.

JAZZ. Yeah. They just wouldn't take her till she was twenty-one cos she wouldn't have been allowed to serve drinks.

> 'S really quiet with just me here though.

RED. Yeah. I bet.

> Jazz, I don't get your dad. I don't get loving someone that much – and just… like a year ago today, I looked on my phone, a year ago today we were all watching *Gladiator*, you, me, Milla, my mum and your dad. And now it's a year later and everything's shit and I don't know why.

JAZZ. Red…

RED. Why would he just cut and run. For no reason.

JAZZ *shrugs*.

Don't just shrug. Is that it, just –

RED *does a caricatured version of* JAZZ*'s shrug*.

JAZZ. I dunno. Maybe you should talk to Milla about this.

RED. Well I never see Milla any more, do I, sounds like I'll never see her again at this rate, and I'm not talking to her, am I, I'm talking to you so I'm asking *you*, *Jazz*, what do *you* think?

JAZZ. But like… they're divorced. That's it. We can't like, do anything about it, so it's not worth me thinking anything.

RED. Really.

JAZZ. I dunno what you want me to say. I mean – if I'm honest – I kind of saw it coming.

Beat.

RED. Okay.

JAZZ. Sorry if that –

RED. No, clearly I'm just stupid. Clearly.

Pause.

Why'd you see it coming?

JAZZ. Er. Don't go mad when I say this okay?

I, uh, saw my dad's porn.

Beat.

RED.…right.

Right.

JAZZ. And like, on its own that doesn't mean anything, like it's gross but, whatever, just – I borrowed his laptop for my PE presentation because it was when PowerPoint kept crashing on the main computer –

RED. When? When was this?

JAZZ. Ages ago. I dunno. Like – September? I dunno. It was only the one time but it was like twenty sites of this… teen girl stuff.

JAZZ sees RED*'s reaction and backtracks.*

Nothing weird, not like, *kids* – but like – 'barely legal' or whatever.

So.

RED. Shit.

JAZZ. Mm.

RED. You're really calm about this, mate, how are you more calm about this than about Col and Hannah?!

JAZZ. Cos I've kinda bleached it out of my brain. I just don't think about it.

RED. That kind of.

Kind of puts everything in a different… light, I guess.

Pause.

Shit.

JAZZ. I'm really sorry but – I have to get to sleep really soon. I'm trying to get up early every morning to run.

RED. Okay.

JAZZ. It's shit but. I kind of have to get in the habit, the camp people said I should.

RED. So what should I do?

Beat. JAZZ *takes a bit too long to make the connection.*

JAZZ. You can sleep here too if you want.

RED. Nah. It's fine.

JAZZ. You can have Milla's bed.

RED. It's fine.

It doesn't count when I make you ask, y'know?

JAZZ *tries to think of a helpful response but before she can:*

Can I have some water before I go? Just in case I feel –
[*sick*] again on the way back.

JAZZ. Oh – one sec –

JAZZ *finds her sports bottle and hands it to* RED, *who takes
a long slug.*

*She holds onto the bottle for a moment, taking in the room
again.*

RED. My mum would *love* this place, y'know.

Beat.

JAZZ. Yeah.

Milla's bed's still there. It's up to you.

RED. I'm just gonna stay here for like... five more seconds.

She stands there longer than that.

Time passes slowly.

3 a.m.

The suburbs

KEESH *and* JAFFA. JAFFA *is playing a video game;* KEESH *is advising.*

JAFFA. Hang on can I use my sniper here?

KEESH. Nah your play style's a bit – up-close for a sniper. They take ages to reload as / well.

JAFFA. Okay, help!

KEESH. Kite them. Kite them.

JAFFA. *How*?

KEESH. This way. No, not – there are enemies that way – back to where you were at the start. You have to run or / they'll –

JAFFA *dies.*

JAFFA. *Nooooo.*

KEESH. Yeah. That happens.

JAFFA. I'm gonna be so annoyed if it takes me back like ten minutes…

JAFFA *shakes his hands around, getting ready to play again while the game loads their last autosave.*

Okay. Cool.

KEESH. Right – so – this you can do.

JAFFA. Yeah.

A small silence as they're both concentrating, transfixed.

KEESH. You can / kite –

JAFFA Yeah – I know –

Pause.

KEESH. Cos you don't wanna be using a pistol when you're right up close, you wanna switch to shotgun.

JAFFA. Okay…

KEESH. And you wanna get into a rhythm of like, shotgun, bam, once or twice, and then you run away and they have to chase after you while you cool down, 'cos otherwise they'll just mêlée on you, okay?

JAFFA. Right –

KEESH. So – close-up – shotgun – RUN AWAY RUN AWAY –

JAFFA. I'm doing it the controls are all – screwy –

KEESH. Yes! Yes! So just check there's nobody –

JAFFA. One more over there –

KEESH. – no don't bother with – just pistol him –

Amazing. Okay so now –

JAFFA. Shh shh shh shh shh –

JAFFA *reads or listens to something new happening in the game.*

What does that mean?

KEESH. You can go back to the underground passage and save her or you can keep going this way and save Julius and he replaces Laya in your party.

JAFFA. Wait, seriously?

KEESH. Yeah, it's like the first big choice you have to make.

JAFFA. So if I go and help Laya I can't actually do the rest of the quest?

KEESH. Yeah.

JAFFA. And if I leave her she's dead? For real?

KEESH. Yeah.

JAFFA. For the whole game?

KEESH. Yeah.

JAFFA. Jeeeesus. So what happens if I save her not Julius?

KEESH. Nobody from his tribe will help you the whole rest of the game.

They'll just get in your face about it.

JAFFA. Okay. Is that… how much help would they / actually.

KEESH. No no no I can't tell you, you just have to choose with what you know now.

A pause while JAFFA *mulls.*

JAFFA. That's not a fair choice though. In real life there'd be a way to do both cos I could just / send –

KEESH. Yeah but in real life you wouldn't be able to spend all this time thinking about it, you'd just have to decide in the moment, so it's not like they're going for realism. In real life no one would just come up and give you the choice between A and B.

JAFFA. Okay here we go. Keesh, are you gonna A – play video games all night or B – do your essay?

KEESH. Oh my god just cos you got to a hard bit.

JAFFA. *Keesh.* It's 3 a.m.

KEESH *looks at her watch, doesn't want to believe it, and compares it to* JAFFA*'s.*

But they both say the same time.

KEESH. That did *not* feel like four hours.

JAFFA. I know.

JAFFA *gets his bag, and dumps out an improbable number of energy drinks.*

KEESH. Thing is though.

JAFFA. What?

KEESH. I have time, I've got the whole of this week.

JAFFA. Yeah, except she wants you to post it to her for Monday.

KEESH (*knowing this is a pathetic excuse*). I don't have a big enough envelope.

JAFFA *reaches inside his bag, brings out a big enough envelope.*

JAFFA. I *brought* you a bloody envelope.

KEESH. How did you do that??

JAFFA. Magic.

JAFFA *takes an energy drink and opens it.*

Come on. Down it.

KEESH *reluctantly does the same.*

KEESH. What's she actually gonna do though? Like, send bailiffs over? It's half-term.

JAFFA. She will ring up your house. And she'll ring early enough that you're still asleep and your mum'll bring the phone to you in bed and you'll have to try and sound like you haven't just woken up. And that *never works.*

KEESH. That just sounds kinda funny to me.

Beat.

JAFFA. And she'll use it an excuse to dick on you when you get back.

Beat.

I promise you'll feel better once you do it.

KEESH. Oh my god. Jaffa. Shut up. Look.

This is gonna sound like an excuse.

JAFFA....right.

KEESH. It's really hard to make myself start when I'll just put loads of effort in and then end up getting like four out of forty like last time. It's all too big and scary now.

Beat.

You know she didn't even like, ask me permission before she read all of it out to the class?

JAFFA. She probably knew you'd say no.

KEESH. Yeah. I shoulda stuck a copyright on it or something. Then I could sue her.

They treat us like shit for being in bottom set.

JAFFA. Keesh…

KEESH. They do! You're not there, they treat us like shit. Or she does, at least.

And I wouldn't be so crap at it if she was a better teacher anyway. Like you remember when I went to go talk to her after we got results for the Russia paper –

JAFFA. *Fuck me*, the Russia paper –

KEESH. And she were like, 'You got the lowest result in the year, lower than the students who have English as a second language' and I wanted to be like, yeah, whose fault is that? It's not like they'd even have let me take History if they knew I were gonna do that bad.

And she's *so nice* to you.

JAFFA. I know. It's crap.

But y'know my last report from her was literally copypasted from someone else's, she called me a 'she' halfway through.

KEESH. Really?

JAFFA. Yeah. 'He is a pleasant and polite pupil who has made satisfactory efforts in History this term. He has learnt to explain her answers and develop them into an argument.'

KEESH. 'Pleasant and polite'.

JAFFA. Yeah, I *know*.

KEESH. Could be worse, I was 'lively'.

Beat.

JAFFA. You want me to put some bird poo in her pigeonhole?

KEESH *can genuinely consider this, or pretend to.*

KEESH. Nah you're all right.

JAFFA. Cos I could. Just write your essay, get a bird to do one on it, then attach a little note saying, 'It's already been shat on, so you don't have to.'

Beat.

KEESH. I just want one night not thinking about it, is all.

JAFFA. Didn't you take the night off from it, like, every single night last week?

KEESH. Yeah but I were still thinking about it – so the week just ran away from me – and I had this like, cold sweat on the whole time from thinking about it. Like feel my hand right now.

JAFFA. I'm not gonna feel your hand.

Beat.

I didn't go to Mog's thing tonight. Cos you said you wanted help.

KEESH. You can get off with Mog any time though.

JAFFA. Yeah, I *definitely* can't.

Pause.

'Specially since now people will probably start going on again about *us* being together.

KEESH (*unable to help herself*). I mean, if you keep bringing me romantic gifts like envelopes, what are people s'posed to think?

Sorry.

I can leave if you want.

JAFFA. Yeah well you're here now, aren't you.

Pause.

I'm gonna get some food.

JAFFA *heads out.*

KEESH *tries to get herself to focus on her history textbook, but gives up after a few moments and chucks it away angrily.*

She hears JAFFA *arguing downstairs with his mum. Freezes a bit to try and make out what they're saying but can't.*

She goes and retrieves the textbook, trying to smooth it out where it got creased. Near where it landed, KEESH *spots a framed photograph, lying face down. She stretches to pick it up and look at it – then laughs out loud.*

JAFFA *comes back with a plastic bag and empties about five packs of strawberry sugar laces out of it.*

KEESH. Jaffa, is that *you*?!

JAFFA. Oh – gimme that back.

KEESH. That is *priceless*, why've you got it up / here?!

JAFFA. *Give* it – my mum were up here last night being like, 'Remember this little boy? What happened to him??'

KEESH. Why? I'd have thought she'd be like, 'Oh, you're doing so well.'

JAFFA. I dunno. I think she thought I were just gonna stay a baby forever.

KEESH. Really?

JAFFA. Well. I think that's it. That's how I feel with the twins, I'm still surprised they can walk.

KEESH. Yeah that's creepy.

Beat.

Did we wake your mum up?

JAFFA. Er – yeah.

KEESH (*whispering*). Sorry.

JAFFA. It's fine.

KEESH (*maybe even whispering still, in a big fake stage-whisper*). I've like completely ruined your night.

JAFFA. No.

Beat.

KEESH. What's your mum worried about?

JAFFA. Uh.

KEESH. Is it to do with the time she was talking to Lou's mum and said she was worried I was rubbing off on you?

JAFFA....I think she's just annoyed because the twins wake her up at like six every day anyway.

KEESH. Has she said anything like that to you about me?

JAFFA. She does like you, I promise. It's loads of other stuff too.

KEESH *stares at* JAFFA *like she doesn't believe him. Because she doesn't.*

But she lets it slide.

Okay.

KEESH *chews on a strawberry lace, looking at the photo again.*

I can't stop looking at your fringe!

JAFFA. Shut up.

KEESH. Is this actually from 2008?

JAFFA. Uh –

KEESH *turns the photo round to show* JAFFA *the date on the back.*

Guess so.

KEESH. Holy shit.

I don't even remember 2008. Or I sort of do but I mostly don't. It's just like bits and pieces and random moments, not a proper like, story.

JAFFA. That's what's wrong with your history essays.

KEESH. Is it?

JAFFA. I dunno. Maybe.

Beat.

KEESH. I'm worried about doing it and now I'm worried about seeing your mum in the morning too. She'll be narked I kept you up all night.

Beat.

Do you know what you're gonna choose?

JAFFA. Do you know what *you're* gonna choose?

KEESH. Yeah well there's a difference between this – (*Pointing at her essay.*) and this – (*Pointing at the console.*)

JAFFA. ?

KEESH. *You* can always do another playthrough after and make the other choice.

Time passes slowly.

4 a.m.

The sticks

A house party.

VJ. Wolfie! Hide me.

WOLFIE. I –

VJ. You have to hide me from Tuss. Please. I'll explain later. Help me, Wolfie, you're my only hope.

WOLFIE. Upstairs loo – window in back – through that, onto the roof.

Beat.

Maybe lock it behind us.

And they're off. They rush through to the loo past various obstacles, and climb out of the window in a really convoluted, difficult way, maybe one having to push the other through.

But they make it, and they emerge onto the roof. VJ *tries to recover.*

VJ. Oh my god. Okay.

WOLFIE. VJ.

VJ. Wow.

WOLFIE. VJ! Can you still hear Tuss?

They both freeze and listen.

VJ. I think we're safe.

Beat.

I never even knew this existed.

WOLFIE. Yeah, I – I've come here a few times.

What's Tuss want with you?

VJ. Uhhh – knows I'm at the point of embarrassing myself.

WOLFIE. Ah.

VJ. I knew you wouldn't judge me. Don't want the same thing to happen again.

I just need to – like – sober up a bit. Fresh air is good.

Beat. VJ *tries to make out the landscape, squinting.*

You can't actually see anything.

WOLFIE. Yeah. I mean it'd just be trees anyway.

VJ. Ugh. Yeah.

What time is it now?

WOLFIE. Uh. Four. Ish.

VJ. First bus in – six hours.

I'm gonna have to stay awake or I'll just sleep through it.

WOLFIE. My mum could give you a lift back with me.

I dunno, like, if you want.

VJ. Nah, don't worry. It's such an awkward place to get to.

WOLFIE. I guess.

VJ. And I'm gonna have an amazing bus nap.

Beat.

Y'know, this conversation is like my last bit of human contact with a sane person for a week.

WOLFIE. Is it?

VJ. Oh yeah. Once I get home, family time all the time.

Pause as WOLFIE *visibly considers saying one thing – then changes her mind.*

WOLFIE. I shoulda brought my jacket out here. I always forget cos I think it's gonna be warm.

I swear this is like the worst party so far. Ever since Lee did the shit in the bath I worry about someone doing that again.

VJ. Wasn't Lee.

WOLFIE. Oh, sure –

VJ. Nah, he stepped up later when I had a fit about no one owning up and he was like 'VJ, I'll clean it up but if I clean it up no one's allowed to say I did it' so I'm not gonna slander him.

WOLFIE. Aw. Okay.

So… we're staying up here till ten?

VJ. We should have got food right?

WOLFIE. I can go find all that cake you brought.

VJ. Nah. Stay here. Sit.

WOLFIE *doesn't have to be told more than that.*

Pause.

My mum always gives me so much stuff to bring cos she's worried I'll look, I dunno, ungrateful.

WOLFIE. I love your mum.

VJ *makes a long, sceptical 'hmmmmm' noise.*

What?

VJ. No, nothing.

She just hates me hanging around and being under her feet but then if I want to go to a party so I can get *out* from under her feet she starts moaning about driving me places and makes all this cake for no reason cos she cares more about what people think of her as a mum than what I actually want.

WOLFIE. You didn't wanna come.

VJ. Well. I wanted to be allowed to come. And even something this boring is better than staying home.

WOLFIE. Do you remember that time when Mac had a party and then afterwards sent us all like / this –

VJ. Like a fucking *bill*! I know! And Alina left her purse behind and he took the money she 'owed' him out of it before giving it back to her.

WOLFIE. Did he actually?

VJ. Yeah.

WOLFIE. What a prick.

VJ. You know what he is?

WOLFIE. He's / rubbo.

VJ. Rubbo. So rubbo.

I can't wait for the day I don't have to see any of them again.

WOLFIE. Really?

> VJ *shrugs*.

That's – Veej, that's really sad.

VJ. No, I just – I don't actually think I'd hang out with most of them if we weren't. You know. Living here.

WOLFIE. Right.

VJ. I don't mean you, but – most people here are just – kind of shit. Even my parents. Everything people care about is shit.

WOLFIE. Er, like what?

VJ. Not you. But. They're fine just living here, in a place in the middle of nowhere where no one's actually doing anything, they're just *raising children*. They don't actually care about anything. And everyone we know is just gonna end up becoming their parents – or worse – and they don't think there's anything wrong with that.

WOLFIE. That's their choice though.

VJ. I know. I know. But for me, personally, for *me*, like, the idea of staying here any longer than I have to or even coming back here ever is – feels like death to me.

WOLFIE. Okay. Wow.

VJ. Sorry. Bit morbid.

WOLFIE. No I get it, I do get that, it's –

> I think you're, I guess, you're clever and so it makes sense. That you feel like that.

VJ. You think I'm clever?

WOLFIE. Er, you know you are.

> VJ *bumps shoulders with* WOLFIE *in a companionable way, as she gets a pen from her pocket.*

VJ. Ahh, Wolfie. You can stay.

> VJ *starts writing her name, doodling little drawings on the roof.*

I dunno. Like… I think I just wanna do something different, I don't wanna do things the way everyone else is doing them but I don't know how and I don't know what I even mean.

Beat.

WOLFIE. I – sometimes feel like –

I get this weird feeling that I've been in the same clothes so long that I'm bursting out of them like the Hulk and when I'm at school I'm like – huge and all of the Year 7s are miniature? And my arms are gonna have to start poking out of the windows and my head's gonna be mashed up against the ceiling cos I'm too – huge for all of it.

VJ is silent, but in a way that means she gets it.

I never talk about this.

VJ. Yeah?

WOLFIE. Well, bit of a downer isn't it.

VJ. No. It's not.

Pause. VJ offers the pen to WOLFIE – who takes it.

She writes her own name on the roof, and the date.

Finally – studiously not looking at VJ – WOLFIE calls VJ by her real name. VJ looks at WOLFIE, slightly surprised by this.

Yeah?

WOLFIE. Sorry I just was gonna say – earlier –

I think you're great, you know.

I've liked you for ages, I think you're brilliant.

Sorry.

Pause.

VJ. Right.

WOLFIE. You're not…

I probably shouldn't have said anything.

VJ. No, it's fine.

WOLFIE. I think I thought that maybe you thought, that time, when I was really drunk and I wouldn't talk to you, that you thought I was being a prick and I just wanted you to know that I wasn't, that I, um, that I actually really like you.

Beat.

Sorry I've just been building up to that for…

Huh.

Pause.

We good?

VJ. Yeah, of course!! Of course we are.

VJ *carefully envelops* WOLFIE *into a hug.*

All right?

Beat.

WOLFIE. Such a shit party.

VJ. I know. The fucking worst.

Pause. WOLFIE *hears noises from inside the house.*

WOLFIE. Are people leaving?

VJ. No. They're just waking up.

5 a.m....

JAFFA. I just about make a decision, though I keep a save just in case I wanna go back.

PEEBS. Me and Epi wander round the beaches and the stone circles a bit.

EPI. It's kinda shit but kinda fun.

WOLFIE. I kinda half do my homework and half-watch TV even though there's nowt on on Sundays –

KEESH. I just think it's not fair to have to wake up this early to go to school.

PEEBS. I know I should make a revision plan but then I look at all these lovely months stretching out on the calendar, and...

RED. Prom is okay. Even though my mum nags at me for choosing the wrong size shoes.

WOLFIE. Results are... fine.

EPI. Sort of what I expected.

KEESH (*to* JAFFA). That's the thing, I keep thinking about how I might just never see you again after September.

VJ. After the first seminar I drag everyone to the pub with me cos I'm like, 'My people! People who are like me!'

JAZZ finishes a run, checks her stopwatch – her time isn't good enough.

JAZZ. Fuck.

KEESH. We try and have each other's backs all the time cos it's either us against customers or us against the area manager.

JAFFA. I'm lugging a load of legal texts through the snow and I just keep on going: two more years and this is done.

EPI. I literally dream about exams now. I dreamt I was taking one and then actually had to wake up and go and take one.

They turn twenty-one

JAZZ. I bust my knee – not allowed to run for months – and I have way too much time to think.

WOLFIE. Way too much time per job application, like, Jesus Christ.

JAZZ. And I start thinking like, maybe this is a sign I should quit while I'm ahead.

EPI. I needed a stamp, which feels so old-timey to say –

VJ. We spend hours mapping glacial valleys –

EPI. And she peeled one off and stuck it on my nose –

VJ. – but once it's dark I keep looking at the lake stretching out for miles –

EPI. – and I could feel myself going really really red.

VJ. And I know it's dangerous, but doggy paddling into the pitch-black coldness of it is incredible.

EPI. – and that's when I knew.

KEESH. There are a few of us that, if we're all together when we're closing, we put on dance music when we clean –

PEEBS. My housemate and me message each other every morning like 'urrrrrrrrr I don't want to get out of bed' which is a weirdly fun ritual.

KEESH. – and then I'll put the same song on my phone when I walk back – and the song'll follow me home – and put me to sleep.

JAFFA. So I told myself: I work as hard as I can and either I A – get on a legal-practice course or B – I don't. And if I don't, I'll do something else.

RED. I'm trying to keep up with things like laundry and stuff but I keep seeing things on my floor. I'm not sure what they are.

JAZZ. Milla really faintly tells me I'm being sensible, all the way from Abu Dhabi.

VJ. This other geoscientist tells me I'm scaremongering and I have to stop myself snatching his stupid mug and smashing it over his head.

WOLFIE. I'm just zoning out while my photocopies print and suddenly it hits me: I was really brave.

VJ. When I quit, on my last day I go and find that guy's mug – write 'PRICK' on the bottom of it in capital letters.

WOLFIE. I spent so long thinking I shouldn't have said anything to her when actually I was really fucking brave.

VJ. And now I've left I wanna do something genuinely important to, like, justify that.

JAZZ. I go and help my dad move house. Again. And after loads of comments about my knee –

RED. And the um the annoying thing is when I have to stop using any social media at all, because it's being monitored.

JAZZ. – which I'd already asked him to shut up about – I just delete his number for a bit.

— We're looking for a donor and we want someone we know.

PEEBS. I might have had too much to drink but that feels like something I could… definitely do.

KEESH. At least when we get made redundant, we all get made redundant together. The end of my last shift is 11 a.m. in the middle of July, and I buy myself a box of ice lollies and eat them on the way home.

Of course everyone's like 'this isn't the end for people working in retail' but. Kind of only a matter of time at this point.

JAFFA. The twins come visit me in London, and afterwards I'm just exhausted. I sort of thought they'd get older and I'd stay the same age.

— If you don't come out of the road I'm gonna have to call someone.

RED. It's fine, I'm walking / to –

— You can't walk to Dover. / You can't walk all the way there.

RED. SSSSSHHHHHH. Shut up. Look – I just – I can't talk about it because / I'm being –

— I just need to – I just want to call someone to make sure you're safe. I promise –

No one is listening to this.

WOLFIE. I take myself to Spain and I take bottles of water and go on really long walks where I feel too… small for all of it.

KEESH. I go to see an eighteen and they wave me through and I have this amazing rush like I've got away with something – then I remember, I'm twenty-seven.

PEEBS. I come and see her occasionally – not stepping on anyone's toes, but, occasionally – and when she was about four I held her up to the mirror and was like – look, okay, you can see you've got my nose, my face shape, my eye-crinkles.

Then I see her a year later and she's got none of those!

They turn thirty

EPI. The day before I turn thirty my dad calls me and – well, tells me what the doctors have said, doesn't actually ask me to come but I – something comes over me and I know I have to step up.

WOLFIE. When I shake her hand for the first time it's like – oh shit. That's it. That feeling again. Hello.

EPI. The whole thing lasts four months.

WOLFIE. Settling in for the long run.

EPI. And then I'm ordering flowers, calling executors, selling his flat, closing the door for the last time and handing over the keys –

WOLFIE. I'm terrified but really fucking happy to feel like this again.

EPI. – and I circle back to Heathrow.

RED. When I come home my mum's really happy to be able to give me a haircut, and I want to make a joke about keeping the scissors away but...

— What have you been up to since the last time I saw you?

KEESH. Oh. Hm. Er.

Well this morning I saw a really good dog.

JAZZ. Hey.

RED *takes* JAZZ's *hand, noting a ring.*

Oh! Yeah. Um. A few years ago.

JAFFA. I buy my mum dinner for her sixtieth, which is great, I'm happy I can do that, and I'm genuinely grateful to her that she gave me so much help to get to that point.

VJ. It's not about not noticing anything day to day – that's not what it's about – like when you're in a plane you don't notice how fast you're going do you, you can only sense acceleration you can't sense velocity –

— V, I kinda just want to watch the film.

VJ. Sorry. It's just on my mind. I'll be quiet.

RED. I think you think I disappear when you don't see me. But I don't. Every second you live, when you're having your cup of tea in the morning and watching telly, I'm living that too. You just don't see it.

JAZZ. Okay.

— There's so much less money in that.

JAFFA. I know. But it's community-oriented.

And it's not that I don't like what I do, in loads of ways it's great, it's… just it's been years now, and…

I don't want to just go on autopilot.

— …

JAFFA. Mum.

— What?

JAFFA. Are you angry with me?

— Of course not. Why would I be angry?

JAFFA.…

KEESH. I'm saving up. I'm trying to be really tight with myself and save it up right now.

VJ. Building a climate model for the next year is pretty straightforward.

KEESH. Cos I don't know what I'll need it for.

VJ. Building one for the next hundred years creates uncertainties.

KEESH. But if there aren't any emergencies I might be able to spend it on something good.

JAZZ. You don't get it, like… the idea of having kids makes me feel terrified.

— Why?

JAZZ. Loads of reasons.

— …

    So that's it, then.

JAZZ. I'm sorry.

— What are you actually worried about?

EPI. Um. I guess. That everything in the future will be just 'more of the same'. Or that things might get worse.

    I don't think about it for a while and then a year's gone by and I'm the same. And then a year goes by and –

They turn forty

PEEBS. Jude corners me at her parents' wedding anniversary and asks what I do when I'm not visiting.

JAZZ. This is what I do when I feel really pissed off and I need some space:

PEEBS. I kind of scramble to think over the past month or year.

JAZZ. I figure out a circular route that feels like it'll take a good long time.

PEEBS. It feels like too much effort to explain tiny things that don't feel that important after they're done.

JAZZ. But then every time I do it, it takes less time and the circle gets smaller.

PEEBS. So I say, I deal with people's problems and then I mostly just go to the pub. And she doesn't respond to that, just keeps eating her candyfloss in a kinda sulky way.

JAZZ. It takes less time to get back to the roads and squares I've already seen.

PEEBS. She just says 'you've got fatter since last year', which, I almost wave my hands spookily and say 'IT'LL HAPPEN TO YOU TOO!' but I don't wanna give her a complex.

JAZZ. Are you angry I didn't come and see you when you were – ?

RED. – oh.

No. You wouldn't have been allowed to.

It woulda been nice if you'd asked.

But it was a long time ago now.

—But what I mean is, how did you just break off from what you were doing like that? How were you brave enough?

JAFFA. Why are you asking me this?

— I dunno. I'm on a track and I feel like it's too late for me to do anything different.

JAFFA You're *thirty*. Both of you are babies.

RED *takes* JAZZ's *hand – no ring.*

JAZZ. Oh – yeah.

RED. I'm sorry.

PEEBS. Jude's doing a long-distance degree and when I'm invited over for Seder she won't shut up about asteroid probe-mining resources. And I love her but *I just don't find it interesting*.

RED. I held off for a while because I was worried I'd pass something on, but she's not me. She's herself. And the other two are so normal it's scary, so. What can you do.

PEEBS. And then she glares at me and says 'oh well I expect that sort of response from people like you' and I'm sorry? People like me?? I have no idea what the hell she means by that.

KEESH.... St Petersburg isn't as cold as I thought it would be.

They turn fifty

VJ. One of my colleagues, one of my friends, we're troubleshooting some code and he makes me a cup of coffee just when I need it and... I don't know. I just look at him differently.

EPI. I go back to the island and sit on the beach near where my school used to be and take some pictures. And I have a conversation in my head with my dad about how he missed out by being in Beijing the whole time.

═══════════════════════════════════════

JAZZ. Do you think it's our parents? Why it's both of us got divorced? And Milla?

RED.... no.

JAZZ. Do you want to go for a run? A walk?

RED. Yeah, let's do that.

They turn sixty

— Are you actually starting a herb garden? Both of you?

WOLFIE. Well. It's what my parents did in *their* sixties.

— That's cos they were retired. And they didn't have to do it in a dome.

═══════════════════════════════════════

— (*to* EPI, *about an instrument*). You used to play, didn't you?

— Did you?!

EPI. Uhh. Yes.

Maybe he even plays a few notes again.

Still can. Still got the muscle memory.

═══

JAFFA. The city I was born near declares bankruptcy and it feels like I just popped out to the shops, left the back door open, and came back to find everything burnt to the ground.

═══

— Would you go back if you could?

PEEBS. Um.

Hm.

═══

VJ. Okay, one of my conditions for staying in this is that we don't spend more than… twenty per cent of the time talking about our health. I don't want to be one of those people.

— You really don't want to hear about my back?

VJ. Oh go on then.

They turn seventy

— I guess it must be scary for you to see so much changing.

JAFFA. Not really.

— No?

JAFFA. I've seen everything change before.

RED. I call my daughter because she's having a tough time with doing normal daily things – talk her through her laundry. And it hurts hearing her struggle, I understand it but my heart hurts for her. And then after I ring off my heart keeps hurting – a sort of stabbing pain – and I think – oh. I see.

VJ. Did I do all right?

— I think so.

They turn eighty

EPI. I keep hearing flight announcements. And making sure I've got everything. For some reason I've got cash in my pocket even though it's been years since we used cash.

And when the plane comes I get on.

WOLFIE. My grandson came up and said, there's going to be a generation ship and I want to go on it.

And I said, what?

JAZZ. Most of the time I don't notice my knee. I don't know if it's stopped hurting… or if everything else has just caught up.

WOLFIE. And he said, a generation ship, we'll go on it and have children and grow old and die on the way to a moon that can support life.

We're going to have a terrarium.

And I said, there's absolutely no way you're doing that, your dad would have a fit.

Although the next time he came he didn't mention it. So maybe I dreamt it.

JAZZ. I don't question when things are different – when someone I thought was alive is dead or someone I thought was dead is alive – I'm not exactly reliable.

PEEBS. I probably would. Go back. For a day or a week or two. Just out of curiosity.

They turn ninety

KEESH. I can tell you where I was born and how I did at school and when I had my first child and when I worked at Sainsbury's and when I was unemployed and the time I went to Russia. But saying it now isn't the same as how it felt at the time. It's not everything.

— That makes sense.

KEESH. I would need more time to tell you everything.

— I think we have to wrap it up now.

KEESH. Don't worry. It was a big ask.

The End (sort of).

...I kinda like it if we leave the play there. I think it leaves us a long way from where we began, with the past irretrievably in the past, in the same way that time does. But like the characters, you too have a choice: A – leave it here, or B – go back to the start in the last few moments. In real life we don't get to go back, which is why I like Option A. But this is theatre, not real life. And anyway, in real life it's only been what, forty-five minutes? An hour? So if Option A doesn't feel right...

Epilogue

KEESH *is finishing her essay, while* JAFFA *sits there timing her.*

KEESH. I hate you. I *hate* you. This is the worst thing I've ever done.

JAFFA. Five seconds.

> KEESH *finishes her sentence, grimaces at the work one last time, and folds the pages up.* JAFFA *holds out the envelope, and* KEESH *slots her essay into it.*

> D'you feel better now?

KEESH. No. Come on, your end of the bargain, you've had ages to think.

JAFFA. All right.

> JAFFA *takes up the console, shows* KEESH *what he's going to pick.*

KEESH. Cool.

> JAFFA *drops his finger from a huge height to make one of the choices in the game.*

JAFFA. That felt a lot less… dramatic than I thought it was gonna be.

KEESH. Same.

> KEESH *cracks open two energy drinks, offers one to* JAFFA.

> Round Two?

> JAFFA *takes it – they clink cans, take a long slug each, and then go back to the game.*

> *The End* (*sort of*).

www.nickhernbooks.co.uk

facebook.com/nickhernbooks

twitter.com/nickhernbooks